The Boston Massacre

The Boston Massacre

Dennis Brindell Fradin

Marshall Cavendish
Benchmark

New York

Dedication

For our dearest family friends, Danny, Goo, Nat, Clare,
and Timmy Newman, with love

Marshall Cavendish Benchmark
99 White Plains Road
Tarrytown, New York 10591-5502
www.marshallcavendish.us

Text and maps copyright © 2009 by Marshall Cavendish Corporation
Map by Rodica Prato

All Internet sites were available and accurate when sent to press.

Library of Congress Cataloging-in-Publication Data
Fradin, Dennis B.
The Boston Massacre / by Dennis Brindell Fradin.
p. cm. — (Turning points in U.S. history)
Summary: "Covers the Boston Massacre as a watershed event in U.S. history, influencing social, economic,
and political policies that shaped the nation's future"—Provided by publisher.
Includes bibliographical references and index.
ISBN 978-0-7614-3010-0
1. Boston Massacre, 1770—Juvenile literature. I. Title.
E215.4.F73 2008
973.3'113—dc22
2007030457

Photo research by Connie Gardner

Cover photo by Bettmann/CORBIS
Cover: A painting by Howard Pyle depicts the British redcoats firing on unarmed Boston colonists.
Title Page: Boston Massacre victims' grave, Old Granary Burying Ground, Boston, Massachusetts

The photographs in this book are used by permission and through the courtesy of: *The Granger Collection:* 12, 14, 27; *North Wind Picture Archive:* 3, 6, 19,
22, 24, 26, 32, 24, 38. *Getty Images:* Hulton Archive, 10, 42-43; *Corbis:* Bettmann, 20, 30; *Art Resource:* New York Public Library, 36.

Editor: Deborah Grahame
Publisher: Michelle Bisson
Art Director: Anahid Hamparian

Printed in Malaysia
1 3 5 6 4 2

Contents

This woodcut depicts an Indian attack on the settlement of Jamestown in the Virginia colony, 1622.

CHAPTER ONE

England's Thirteen Colonies

England settled Virginia, its first **colony** in what is now the United States, in 1607. Between that year and 1733, England settled or took over twelve other American colonies: Massachusetts, New Hampshire, New York, Connecticut, Maryland, Rhode Island, Delaware, Pennsylvania, North Carolina, New Jersey, South Carolina, and Georgia.

For many years the American colonists got along well with their British rulers. The colonists called Britain the Mother Country. People in England valued the thirteen colonies as important possessions.

The Americans even helped the Mother Country fight its wars. For example, from 1754 to 1763, Britain fought France for control of North

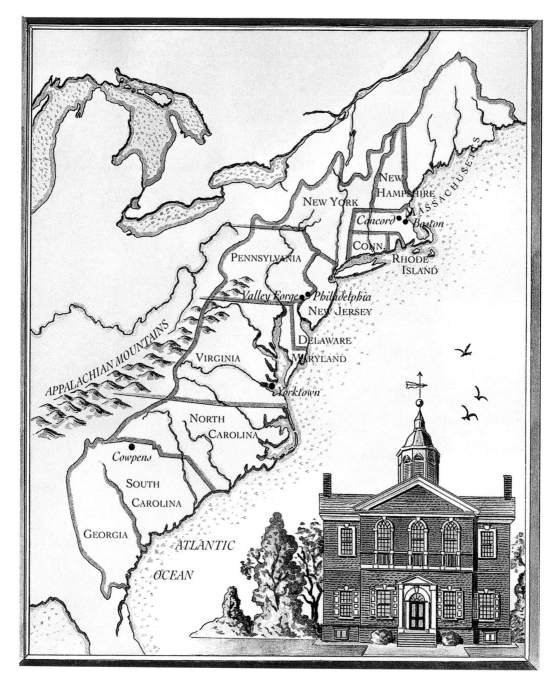

England's thirteen American colonies, settled between 1607 and 1733.

America. Many American Indians helped France, so this conflict is known as the French and Indian War. Thousands of American colonists fought on the British side. Thanks partly to the colonists' help, the British won the French and Indian War.

The French and Indian War (1754–1763) was fought between Britain and France to gain control of North America.

CHAPTER TWO

The Americans Say No to Taxes

The Mother Country had beaten the French, but the British faced a **crisis**. Fighting the French and Indian War had cost Britain a fortune. After the war, Britain had **debts** that would equal many billions of dollars today.

The British government decided to **tax** the American colonists to help pay its bills. Britain's **parliament** passed the Stamp Act, its first major tax on the Americans, in 1765. The Stamp Act required colonists to purchase special tax stamps. These stamps were to be placed on paper goods such as newspapers and legal **documents**. Throughout the thirteen colonies, Americans **protested** the Stamp Act. They thought it was unfair for Britain

Colonists in the public square are shown reading news about the Stamp Act.

to make them pay its debts—especially after they had helped win the French and Indian War.

Boston, Massachusetts, quickly became the colonists' most **rebellious** town. Bostonians James Otis and Samuel Adams earned reputations as two of America's leading rebels. Otis popularized the saying "Taxation without representation is **tyranny**!" This saying meant that Americans were not part of the British parliament, so Britain had no right to tax them. Soon protesters in all thirteen colonies were chanting the saying.

Adams wrote many letters to newspapers to protest the Stamp Act. He also organized a group of several hundred men from the Boston area. This group became known as the Sons of Liberty. Under Adams's leadership, the Sons of Liberty destroyed British officials' homes and **rioted** in the streets.

Parliament **repealed** the Stamp Act in 1766, partly because of all the rebellion happening in Boston. Still, Britain would not give up on taxing the Americans. In 1767 Parliament passed new tax laws called the Townshend Acts. These laws taxed paint, lead, paper, glass, and tea brought into the thirteen colonies.

Once again, the colonists protested. Once again, Boston was the most rebellious town. At Adams's urging, Massachusetts began a campaign

A Separate People

Taxes were not the only reason that Americans became rebellious in the 1760s. By that time, many colonial families had lived in America for more than a century. Most colonists had never even seen England. They felt less and less loyalty to the Mother Country with each passing year. Besides, some colonists had come from other countries such as Germany, the Netherlands, France, and Sweden. The colonists had begun to think of themselves as a separate people—Americans— who deserved their own nation.

Angry Bostonians are shown using the cruel punishment method of tarring and feathering.

to **boycott** British goods, or stop buying them completely. This would cause British merchants to lose a lot of money. The colonists hoped the boycott would convince Parliament to repeal the new taxes. Other colonies followed the lead of Massachusetts and began boycotting British goods.

In Boston, the Sons of Liberty sent gangs of boys to break the windows of merchants who kept doing business with England. The boys also placed signs that said "IMPORTER" outside shops that ignored the boycott. The Sons of Liberty **seized** some importers and coated them with hot tar and feathers.

Women joined the growing rebellion at about this time. In many American towns, women's groups called the Daughters of Liberty pledged to boycott British goods. Instead they made homespun clothing and brewed homemade tea for their families.

Boston Harbor was a busy thoroughfare for people and goods in the 1700s.

CHAPTER THREE

British Soldiers in Boston

Bostonians continued their rebellious ways. In spring 1768 a British tax official boarded the *Liberty*. This ship belonged to wealthy Bostonian John Hancock. The official tried to inspect the ship to see if anyone was breaking a British law. Hancock had his men lock the official in a ship cabin. The British seized the *Liberty* to punish Hancock.

Hancock was one of Boston's most popular leaders. About five hundred angry Bostonians struck back at the British. They attacked two British officials who had helped seize the *Liberty*. The mob threw bricks at the officials and burned a boat belonging to one of them.

John Hancock

John Hancock (1737–1793) was born in Braintree, Massachusetts. His father, a minister, died when John was only seven. His mother could not afford to raise John, so he went to live with his wealthy uncle and aunt in Boston. Hancock's uncle left him a fortune. He became one of the richest men in Massachusetts at the age of twenty-seven.

In the days of the American Revolution, most wealthy Americans sided with England. They did not want things to change. Hancock was different. At Samuel Adams's urging, Hancock poured his heart—and his money—into the struggle for independence. He spent so much money on the American cause that some Bostonians joked, "Samuel Adams writes the letters and John Hancock pays the postage."

In the "*Liberty* affair," Hancock had his men lock a British tax agent in his ship cabin. This was a key event leading to the Boston Massacre. Hancock later served as president of the colonists' revolutionary government, the Continental Congress. In this role, he was the first person to sign the Declaration of Independence on July 4, 1776. To this day, a signature is often called a John Hancock.

Hancock was elected first governor of the state of Massachusetts in 1780. He held the office for eleven years.

The British decided to end the rebellion in Boston. They hoped the rest of America would fall in line, too. In late 1768 British troops arrived in Boston Harbor. On October 1 the soldiers came ashore in a threatening manner. Cannons on the British ships boomed. Seven hundred troops in red coats marched into Boston with their **muskets** on their shoulders.

A Son of Liberty named Paul Revere left his silversmith shop and watched the British troops enter Boston. Revere became angry. He wrote, "[They] marched with **insolent**

British redcoats marched into Boston with much fanfare, to the disgust of many of its citizens.

parade, drums beating, fifes playing, up King Street, each soldier having received sixteen rounds of powder and ball." Revere's last remark means that each soldier had enough ammunition to fire sixteen musket shots.

Paul Revere

Paul Revere was the son of a Boston silversmith. He attended school until the age of thirteen, and then he went to work for his father. By the time his father died five years later, Revere was skilled enough to take charge of the silversmith shop.

Revere was married twice—his first wife died young—and was the father of sixteen children. The silversmith shop did not provide enough money for Revere's large family. Revere made more money by engraving pictures, making false teeth, and designing picture frames.

Revere made cannons for the American army. He also designed and printed the first paper money in the United States.

Paul Revere (1735–1818)

More and more British soldiers arrived. Soon the number of redcoats was four thousand. Boston's entire population was roughly 16,000 at the time. This means there was one British soldier for every four Bostonians.

The redcoats tried to scare the Bostonians. They aimed cannons at important places such as the Old State House, where the Massachusetts **legislature** met. They stopped Bostonians on the streets and demanded to know where they were going. John Adams, Samuel's cousin, wrote that the redcoats marched regularly near his home.

The Bostonians showed the redcoats what they thought of them. Samuel Adams wrote a letter to the *Boston Gazette*. He advised Bostonians to "resist this tyranny." Children followed the redcoats around and called them lobsterbacks. They threw eggs, snowballs, and even rocks at the soldiers.

Thousands of soldiers mixed with thousands of angry citizens. The mixture of soldiers with angry citizens was like a powder keg. By 1769 everyone knew it was just a matter of time before the situation exploded.

James Otis is shown reacting violently to a rude remark.

CHAPTER FOUR

Violence Breaks Out

Violence began to increase in Boston. One of the first incidents involved the man who had popularized the saying "Taxation without representation." James Otis was mentally disturbed. His moods went back and forth between joy and depression. Otis entered the British Coffee House on the night of September 5, 1769. He began arguing with British soldiers, sailors, and officials.

Suddenly, the oil lamps were put out. In the darkness Otis was attacked with swords until blood gushed from his head. Otis's wounds healed, but the attack seemed to destroy his mental health. Otis stopped contributing to the American cause.

The attack on Otis sparked strong hatred toward the British. A few months later, another event made things even worse. In early 1770 a group of boys painted pictures on a board to make fun of merchants who still did business with England. On February 22 they placed the board and an IMPORTER sign outside a merchant's shop.

Boston was also home to a number of Loyalists—Americans who sided with England instead of their fellow colonists. A Loyalist named Ebenezer Richardson tried to remove the board and the IMPORTER sign. The boys saw what Richardson was doing and pelted him with rocks.

Colonists had little tolerance for Loyalists and sometimes forced them out of town.

Richardson rushed home, grabbed his gun, and fired out his window at the boys. Two of them were severely wounded. Christopher Snider, who was only eleven years old, died of his wounds.

A large group of furious Bostonians broke into Richardson's home and dragged him to prison. Richardson was found guilty of murder, but Thomas Hutchinson, governor of Massachusetts, refused to sign the execution paper. King George III later **pardoned** Richardson and released him from prison.

Like the Otis attack, the Snider shooting set the stage for a far more violent event. The worst was yet to come for Boston.

Colonists in Boston held meetings to discuss the problem of redcoats in their town.

CHAPTER FIVE

A Snowball Fight

Becomes a Massacre

The redcoats did more to anger the Bostonians. They got part-time jobs. This meant fewer jobs were available for Boston's citizens. On Friday, March 2, 1770, a British soldier went to apply for a job at a rope-making store called John Gray's Ropewalk. A rope maker said he knew of a job for the redcoat. The soldier asked what the job involved. The rope maker insulted him by saying, "You can clean out my [toilet]!"

The redcoat went to his **barracks** and convinced a few soldiers to return to the Ropewalk. They went to pay back the insult. The rope makers were waiting—with wooden clubs. They beat up the British troops that day and again the next day when some redcoats arrived seeking revenge once more. March 4 was a Sunday, so the two sides stopped fighting. However, the redcoats vowed that the battle was not over.

Monday, March 5, was snowy, but the clouds disappeared that afternoon. By nightfall, Boston looked peaceful beneath a first-quarter moon. The peaceful appearance was deceiving, however. That evening, groups of redcoats shoved Bostonians on the streets. Many townspeople came out of their homes looking for trouble.

On King Street, a crowd made up partly of boys approached a group of redcoats. They called the soldiers names and hit them with stones. The redcoats were ordered to return to their barracks. The crowd then turned its attention to a sentinel, or guard, outside the British customhouse (a tax-collecting building) on King Street. They smacked the redcoat with snowballs and dared him to fire his gun at them.

"Lobsterback!" Boston's boys fearlessly ridiculed British soldiers.

"If you come near me," threatened the terrified guard, "I will blow your brains out! Stand off!"

Meanwhile, a servant hurried to the nearby barracks. "They are killing the sentinel!" the servant reported. This was an **exaggeration**. Nobody was killing the guard.

British captain Thomas Preston rushed out with several men to defend the guard. Captain Preston's troops included one or two men who had been beaten at the Ropewalk. They were eager for revenge. As the redcoats loaded their muskets, the crowd attacked them with snowballs and insults. Then, suddenly, a big object struck a soldier and knocked him down.

"Fire!" someone shouted. Nobody knows who said it. Maybe Captain Preston made the order. Perhaps a Bostonian was daring the British to shoot. What we do know is that the British soldiers responded. The next moment British bullets were flying. American bodies started dropping in the blood-splattered snow.

The shooting stopped, and three men on the American side lay dead. One was Crispus Attucks. He was believed to be an escaped slave from an inland town. Another was Sam Gray, a rope worker at John Gray's Ropewalk. The third was James Caldwell, a sailor. Eight other men were wounded. Six of them recovered, but seventeen-year-old Samuel Maverick died the next morning. Patrick Carr also died after about a week. That raised the American death toll to five.

Paul Revere's 1770 engraving has appeared in books and exhibits hundreds of times.

People told different stories about the fight. British supporters said the Bostonians started the King Street brawl. On the other hand, Americans thought the redcoats used the tossing of a few snowballs as an excuse to kill defenseless people.

Rebel leader Samuel Adams knew the Bostonians were partly to blame for the violence. Still, he saw an opportunity to get more people against the British. Adams wanted people to think of the brawl as the **slaughter** of innocent Americans. He named the event the Boston **Massacre**. He also asked his friend Paul Revere to create an engraving of the event. The engraving made the British soldiers look like murderers.

The King Street clash went down in history as the Boston Massacre. Adams twisted the truth very well. To this day, most people think the event happened exactly as Adams described it.

This illustration shows Samuel Adams making demands during a meeting with the governor after the Boston Massacre.

CHAPTER SIX

Aftermath of the Boston Massacre

The Boston Massacre was a turning point in the conflict between Britain and the thirteen colonies. Previously, the main issue had been taxes. Now, the split between the colonists and their British rulers deepened. Some Americans even talked about forming their own **independent** country. The Boston Massacre helped make this idea a reality.

At a huge meeting the day after the massacre, Bostonians decided that the redcoats must leave their town. Samuel Adams was appointed to tell Governor Hutchinson. Adams delivered a threat. If Hutchinson did not order the redcoats to leave, the Americans would drive them out. Governor Hutchinson **reluctantly** ordered the British soldiers out of

Boston. People in Britain were outraged. Since when did colonists tell their rulers what to do?

Meanwhile, Captain Thomas Preston and eight other soldiers were arrested for being part of the Boston Massacre. People in Britain expected the Americans to convict the redcoats of murder and hang them. Samuel Adams had other plans, however. He wanted to show the world that Americans placed justice before revenge. He arranged for the redcoats to have fine lawyers. Josiah Quincy and John Adams, Samuel's cousin, defended the soldiers at their trial.

Adams and Quincy did excellent legal work at the trial. None of the redcoats were found guilty of murder. Captain Preston and six of his men were found not guilty, and they were freed. The other two soldiers were found guilty of **manslaughter**, a less serious charge than murder. Their sentence was much less harsh than hanging. The soldiers were branded on the thumb with a hot iron.

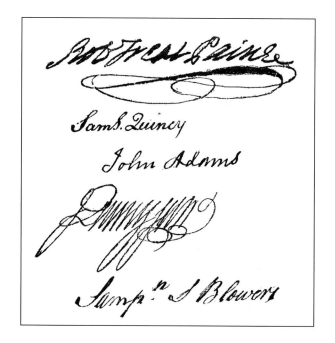

Signatures of lawyers for both sides in the Boston Massacre trial

John Adams

John Adams was born near Boston in Braintree, Massachusetts, in 1735. After graduating from Harvard University, he became a schoolteacher. Adams later said that he learned everything he needed to know about human nature from his students. Teaching was difficult, however. He gave it up after a year and turned to law.

In one of Adams's most famous legal cases, he successfully defended the redcoats involved in the Boston Massacre. He was worried that his countrymen would hate him for it. Many people did disagree with his actions, but others admired his sense of fairness and his legal skill.

Later, while in the Continental Congress, John and his cousin Samuel helped George Washington become the commander of the revolutionary army. John helped Thomas Jefferson write the Declaration of Independence. He was also one of the signers of the document.

From 1789 to 1797, Adams was the first vice president of the United States. After George Washington left office, Adams served as the country's second president from 1797 to 1801.

By a remarkable coincidence, ninety-year-old Adams and eighty-three-year-old Jefferson died on the same day. It was a very special day—July 4, 1826, the fiftieth birthday of the United States.

Naming a New Country

In the years following the Boston Massacre, the people of Boston held a Massacre Day memorial on or near March 5. One highlight of the event was a patriotic speech. On March 5, 1774, the fourth anniversary of the massacre, John Hancock was the speaker. Hancock said that the colonists should form a new country called the United States of America. This is one of the first times the name was proposed. Samuel Adams might have been secretly responsible for this suggestion, however. Adams's daughter Hannah later said that her father wrote Hancock's speech.

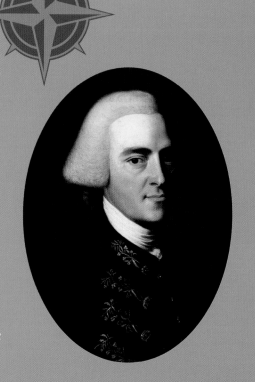

John Hancock (1737–1793)

Britain became even more determined to make the colonists obey their Mother Country. In 1773 Parliament passed the Tea Act, a new law taxing tea. Again, the colonists rebelled. Americans in many towns dumped and burned British tea at what they called tea parties. Boston led the way with its famous Boston Tea Party of December 16, 1773.

The Boston Tea Party is often depicted in broad daylight, yet it occurred at night with just a thin crescent moon in the sky.

Minutemen stand their ground as British soldiers advance during the Battle of Lexington.

War or Scrambled Eggs?

The Revolutionary War began in Lexington, Massachusetts, on April 19, 1775. If not for a broken egg, it might have begun six weeks earlier. March 5, 1775, was a Sunday, so that year's Massacre Day memorial was held one day late. On March 6, 1775, patriots gathered at a Boston church. Dr. Joseph Warren made a fiery speech against the British. About forty fully armed redcoats wanted to cause trouble, so they also came to the church. The plan was for a redcoat to throw a raw egg at Warren as he spoke. That would be the signal for the British soldiers to capture Warren, Samuel Adams, and John Hancock.

If the British had done this, it might have led to a battle. However, the signal was never given. The soldier with the egg fell as he entered the church, injured his knee, and broke the egg. A British newspaper later reported that only this accident kept the redcoats from trying to arrest the three American leaders.

Finally, war between Britain and the American colonies broke out on April 19, 1775. It started with the Battle of Lexington, a town outside Boston. During the battle, the British tried to capture Samuel Adams and John Hancock. The war for American independence had begun.

Glossary

barracks—Buildings used to house soldiers.

boycott—An organized plan to refuse to buy certain goods in an effort to get better treatment.

debts—Money or things that are owed to someone.

colony—A settlement built by a country beyond its borders.

crisis—A severe problem or emergency.

documents—Important papers.

exaggeration—An overstatement.

importer—Someone who brings in goods from another country.

independent—Free or self-governing.

insolent—Insulting; bold.

legislature—A group of people that makes laws.

manslaughter—The unlawful killing of a person without planning it ahead of time.

massacre—The killing of many defenseless people.

muskets—Long, heavy guns used during the American Revolution.

pardoned—Released from punishment; set free.

parliament—A type of legislature.

protested—Spoke or acted against something.

rebellious—Fighting against authority.

reluctantly—Without really wanting to.

repealed—Took back; canceled.

rioted—Behaved violently in public.

seized—Took or stole.

slaughter—The killing of many people.

tax—To charge and collect money for public purposes.

tyranny—Unjust and oppressive power.

Timeline

1607—England settles Virginia, its first permanent American colony

1620—The Pilgrims begin settling Massachusetts, England's second American colony

1733—England's thirteenth American colony, Georgia, is established

1754–1763—Britain wins the French and Indian War with the help of American colonists

1765—Britain's parliament passes the Stamp Act; the Sons of Liberty and other colonists stage protests

1766—Parliament repeals the Stamp Act

1767—Parliament passes the Townshend Acts, taxing many goods brought into the thirteen colonies

1768—**June:** British soldiers seize John Hancock's ship, the *Liberty*; a riot occurs in Boston **October 1:** The British send troops into Boston

1769—**September 5:** American patriot James Otis is attacked in Boston's British Coffee House

1607   *1765*   *1768*

1770—February 22: Loyalist Ebenezer Richardson shoots and severely wounds two American boys; Christopher Snider later dies
March 5: The Boston Massacre occurs; Parliament repeals all the Townshend Acts except the tax on tea

1773—May 10: Parliament passes the Tea Act
December 16: Americans destroy British tea at the Boston Tea Party

1774—September 5: The First Continental Congress opens in Philadelphia

1775—April 19: The Revolutionary War begins in Lexington and Concord, Massachusetts
May 10: The Second Continental Congress opens in Philadelphia

1776—July 4: The Declaration of Independence is approved

1783—The Americans win the Revolutionary War

1970—Americans celebrate the two-hundredth anniversary of the Boston Massacre, which helped set off the American Revolution

1770

1776   *1970*

Further Information

B O O K S

Fradin, Dennis. *Samuel Adams: The Father of American Independence.* New York: Clarion, 1998.

Kjelle, Marylou Morano. *John Hancock.* Hockessin, DE: Mitchell Lane, 2006.

Santella, Andrew. *The Boston Massacre.* Danbury, CT: Children's Press, 2004.

Somervill, Barbara A. *The Massachusetts Colony.* Chanhassen, MN: The Child's World, 2004.

W E B   S I T E S

This Web site focuses on the Boston Massacre trials:
http://www.law.umkc.edu/faculty/projects/ftrials/bostonmassacre/
bostonmassacre.html

This Web site explains the role Crispus Attucks played in the Boston Massacre:
http://www.pbs.org/wgbh/aia/part2/2p24.html

This Web site contains a behind-the-scenes look at Paul Revere's famous Boston Massacre engraving:
http://www.earlyamerica.com/review/winter96/massacre.html

Bibliography

Butterfield, L.H., ed. *Diary and Autobiography of John Adams.* Cambridge, MA: Harvard University Press, 1961.

Canfield, Cass. *Samuel Adams's Revolution.* New York: Harper & Row, 1976.

Fischer, David Hackett. *Paul Revere's Ride.* New York: Oxford University Press, 1994.

Fowler, William M. *The Baron of Beacon Hill: A Biography of John Hancock.* Boston: Houghton Mifflin, 1980.

Hall-Quest, Olga W. *Guardians of Liberty: Sam Adams and John Hancock.* New York: Dutton, 1963.

Labaree, Benjamin Woods. *Colonial Massachusetts: A History.* Millwood, NY: KTO Press, 1979.

Lewis, Paul. *The Grand Incendiary: A Biography of Samuel Adams.* New York: Dial, 1973.

Wells, William V. *Life and Public Services of Samuel Adams.* Boston: Little, Brown, 1866.

Zobel, Hiller B. *The Boston Massacre.* New York: Norton, 1970.

Index

Page numbers in **boldface** are illustrations.

About the Author

Dennis Fradin is the author of 150 books, some of them written with his wife, Judith Bloom Fradin. Their book for Clarion, *The Power of One: Daisy Bates and the Little Rock Nine*, was named a Golden Kite Honor Book. Another of Dennis's well-known books is *Let It Begin Here! Lexington & Concord: First Battles of the American Revolution*, published by Walker. Other recent books by the Fradins include *Jane Addams: Champion of Democracy* for Clarion and *5,000 Miles to Freedom: Ellen and William Craft's Flight from Slavery* for National Geographic Children's Books. Their current project for National Geographic is the *Witness to Disaster* series about natural disasters. *Turning Points in U.S. History* is Dennis's first series for Marshall Cavendish Benchmark. The Fradins have three grown children and five grandchildren.